A Sense of
Shabbat

by
Faige Kobre

Torah Aura Productions
Los Angeles, California

For "Imma" Kobre (of blessed memory)
who loved Shabbos and her grandchildren

ACKNOWLEDGMENTS: I'd like to give thanks to the various people that have pushed, prodded or encouraged or otherwise helped me in seeing this book to its fruition. First of all Bella Rubashkin for helping plant the seed; Rivka Behar and Ruth Mushnikow at the Board of Jewish Education; Ken Wittenberg at Empire State College; Anne Marie Mott at Bank St. College; Adina Schwimmer and Esther Fischer from Magen David Yeshiva; My parents, my husband, and all the children who have allowed me to photograph them (some of whom are almost graduating high school).

Text and Photographs copyright © 1989 Faige Kobre

Library of Congress Cataloging-in-Publication Data

Kobre, Faige
    A sense of Shabbat/Faige Kobre
      p. cm.
    Summary: Text and photos illustrate the process of getting ready for and celebrating Shabbat as it is experienced through our five senses.
    ISBN 0–933873–44–1 (pbk.)
    1. Sabbath—Juvenile literature.   [1. Sabbath.]   I. Title.
BM685.K57   1989
296.4'1—dc20   89-40361 CIP AC

First Edition

MANUFACTURED IN THE UNITED STATES OF AMERICA

Torah Aura Productions
4423 Fruitland Avenue
Los Angeles, California 90058
(800) BE-TORAH   (213) 585-7312

Shabbat.

Shabbat is coming!

Shabbat is coming again.

But what is Shabbat?

3

Shabbat is a special day for Jewish people.

It comes every week on Friday night when it's still light outside and leaves the next night when the sky is dark.

Shabbat is
one whole night
and one whole day.

Shabbat.
Shabbat is coming.

Shabbat
is coming soon!

Quick! Take out the dirty candlesticks. Take out a clean old rag. Take out that creamy soft polish and

MUSH! SQUISH!
SLUSH! SWISH!

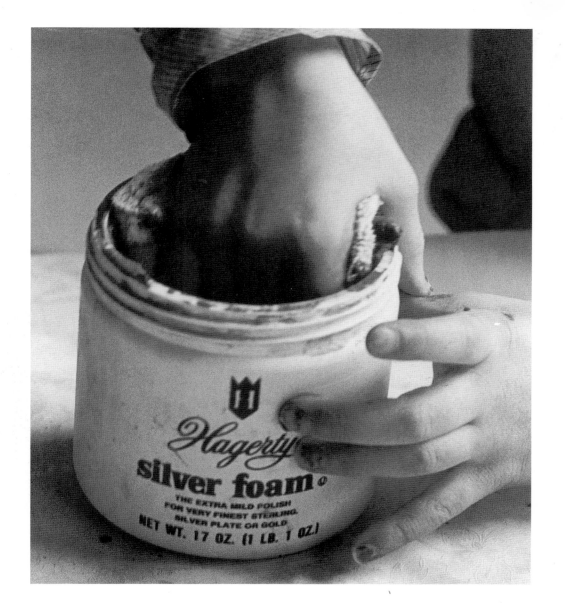

7

Now put away that old spotted rag

and look at those shiny, smooth, silvery candlesticks.

Now they are ready for Shabbat.

<u>H</u>allah! Let's make <u>h</u>allah.

Prepare the dough. Pour the ingredients.

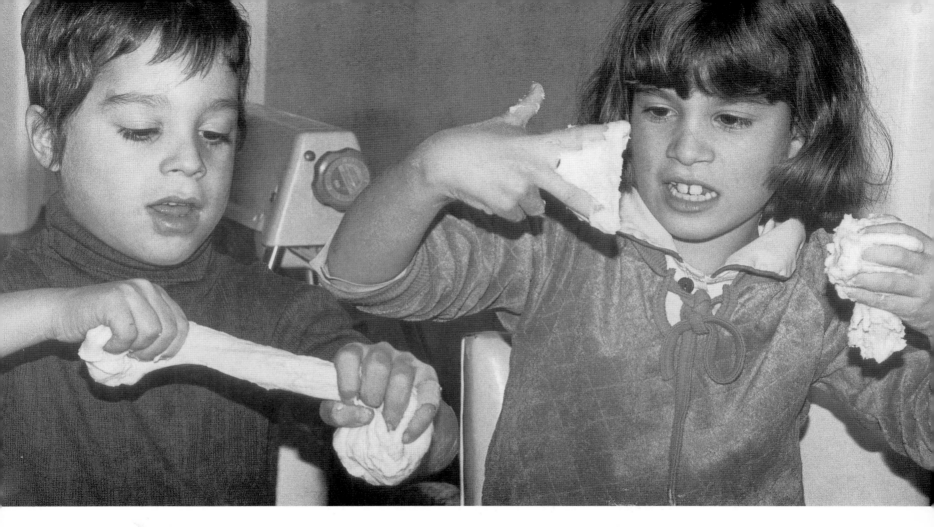

Pound and press, pinch and knead.

Watch the
dough
rise
and rise
and rise.

12

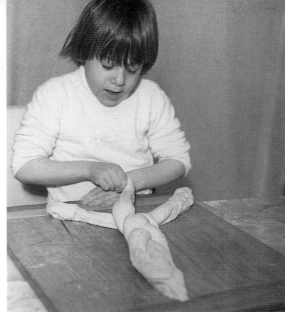

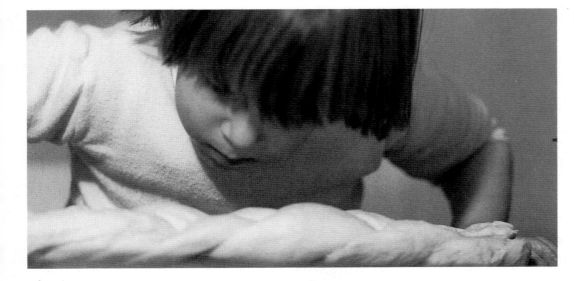

Now,

braid the dough.

13

Next let's bake it. When it's done, we can smell it. But we have to wait for Shabbat to taste it.

14

Watch the clean white tablecloth whisk onto the table. Put the

15

crusty, crunchy <u>h</u>allot in their place.

Set the
white candles
in the
gleaming
candlesticks.

16

Shabbat
is just about here.

Lift your hands.
Light the lovely   17
candles.

18

Quietly, let's welcome Shabbat.

"Hello Shabbat! We were waiting for you."

Shabbat is here at last.

The Shabbat wine
slurps
and slips
and glides
into the cup.

It almost
spills over.

20

Listen!
Then say,
"Amen," to
Kiddush, the
blessing over   21
the wine.

Taste the cool, sweet, delicious Kiddush wine.

Feel it slide down your throat.

Wash your hands. Feel the cold, tingling water gushing and rushing over them.

23

Then the hallah.

Wait!

First let's make Ha-motzi and then

24

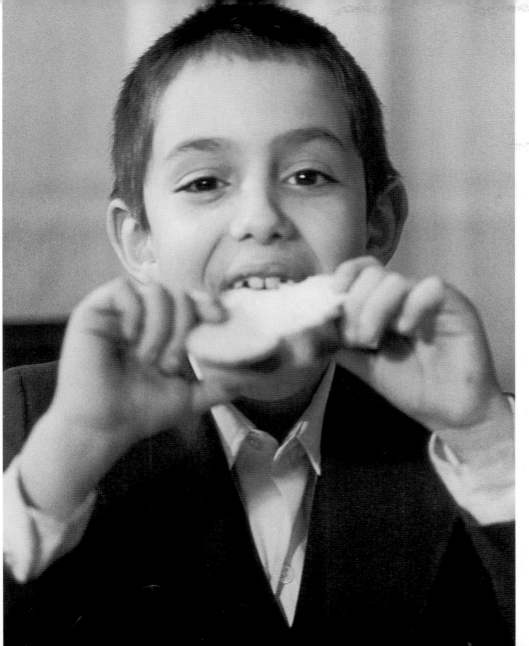

take
big,
gooey
bites
into
soft,
chewy
<u>ha</u>llah.

25

On Shabbat,
it is so nice to be all
together,
to stay up late,
to have no school,
to sing Shabbat songs,

and to eat all those special Shabbat foods.

Shabbat is a whole day, but now it is almost over.
It is dark outside. Shabbat is ending.

Time to light the Havdalah candle.

Watch out for the wax!

Don't let it drip.

29

Hold the wine glass carefully.

The wine is spilling over the top!

See the

flickering light   31

in your fingernails.

Smell.
Sniff
the
sweet
smelling
cloves.